To Gerard, w

R. T. Fishall

[Alias Patrick Moore]

1993 February 17

The Twitmarsh File

The Twitmarsh File
or, the Barmy Army

R.T. FISHALL

SIDGWICK & JACKSON
LONDON

First published in Great Britain in 1985
by Sidgwick and Jackson Limited

Illustrations by Harry North

ISBN 0-283-99280-0

Printed in Great Britain by
Anchor Brendon Limited, Tiptree, Essex
for Sidgwick and Jackson Limited
1 Tavistock Chambers, Bloomsbury Way
London WC1A 2SG

Contents

1

Bureaucrats Revisited: The Tomlinson Effect

Some months ago I read a report about a fascinating underground nuclear shelter at Taunton. It had been set up by the Somerset County Council, and was intended for up to a hundred local government administrators, who could go there as soon as some unfriendly person lobbed an atom bomb into the West Country. It had two chemical toilets, and the only water supply came from a large tank on the seventh floor of an adjoining block of flats.

This intrigued me, because I had already been undertaking some research into the world of bureaucracy. As readers of my earlier work may recall, it began in 1981, with a letter from Mr K. Whitmarsh of the Southern Gas Company threatening me with instant legal action over non-payment of a £10 repair bill to the central heating in my home. As this system is dependent wholly upon oil, the situation was fraught with interest at once, and the subsequent correspondence with Mr Whitmarsh – now known widely and no doubt affectionately as Twitmarsh – confirmed my views that a whole store of hidden knowledge remained to be tapped. I found that Twitmarshes abound in almost all official departments. It may even be said that they cluster as thickly as woodworms in an old barn, and that they nibble away at the ratepayers'

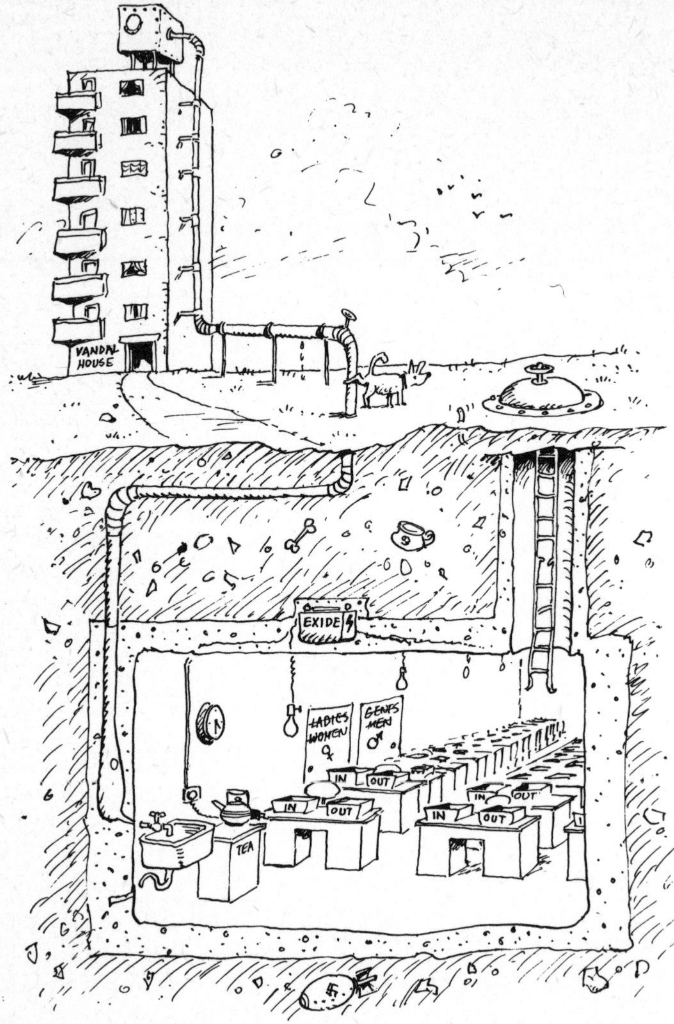
VANDAL HOUSE
EXIDE
LADIES
WOMEN
GENTS
MEN
IN
OUT
IN
OUT
IN
OUT
IN
OUT
TEA

money every whit as effectively as the most well-trained woodworm can devour an ancient beam.

After the publication of my book, I had a letter from a Mr Roy Tomlinson, from the Land Registry in Nottingham, who is a member of the Society of Civil and Public Servants. Mr Tomlinson did not number among my greatest admirers, and he was incensed at the book, which he described as vicious and mischievous. Following my own set of FLs or Fundamental Laws, I naturally returned his letter in an unstamped envelope, with a staple through the middle (FL No. 7). Having paid 25p to get it back, Mr Tomlinson took me to task in *Opinion*, the Society's Journal. His letter, published in the issue of February 1983, left no room for doubt about his feelings. For example, he objected to my comment that 'all Civil Servants earn a full week's wages for a full day's work'; he commented upon my 'cheap and easy' remarks, 'puerile pranks', 'very limited talent' etc., and referred to the sad plight of Inland Revenue officers, who were 'working under pressure with an insufficient complement due to present Government cut-backs'. He also objected to my remarks which cast aspersions upon 'the integrity of a body of people who are, despite your reluctance to accept the fact, in respectable employment, carrying out the instructions of their employers'. Mr Tomlinson's letter was carried under the heading *This Man Wants to Make a Misery of Your Life*, and was accompanied by pictures both of myself and of the cover of the book.

Predictably, the effect was to shoot the book straight

into the bestseller list, as almost every Civil Servant in the realm seemed to dash out and buy a copy. I wrote to Mr Tomlinson, expressing my most grateful thanks, but for some reason he didn't reply. I must therefore pay public tribute to him for his generous help.

The only other critical letter I had was from a Mr Athans, who is Welsh, and who complained about my statement that 'most Twitmarshes are adept at murdering the English language', and wanted to know why I had mentioned English rather than Welsh. He added that if there were six hundred angels in Westminster they would still be English angels, unable to understand the mind of Wales. Looking at the Houses of Parliament, I frankly doubt whether they contain any angels, English or otherwise, but of course I took Mr Athans' point. I replied to him in Icelandic. He responded by answering me in French, which is a language I can actually read without difficulty!

On the credit side, I had some very helpful tips. Believe it or not, the ploy which seems to be particularly successful is that of the humble staple, attached to a tax cheque or something equivalent (inserted right through one's signature, naturally). I am told that one VAT computer was jammed for at least a day after a staple found its way into the machine's innards. Another hint, which I omitted originally because I hadn't thought of it, is that of the Immediate Receipt. Send your cheque to the Twitmarsh concerned, taking care to obtain proof of posting, and request a receipt within seven days. If you don't get it (as you probably won't), cancel the cheque and write asking confirmation that your original letter has not been received – naturally quoting a fictitious reference number. Apparently Twitmarshes have yet to find the counter to this.

However, be very careful to make sure that you have proof of posting, because it is true that there has been a significant change of attitude among some Twitmarshes during the past year or two. In particular there has been an increase in the number of Bureaukrauts. So always be on your guard, and leave no loophole.

Gas Boards continue to be absolutely stuffed with Twitmarshes. Consider the case of Mr Hugh Sinclair, of Stretford in Manchester. He was accused of fiddling his meter, and his gas supply was cut off. A subsequent inspection showed that the North West Gas Board had fitted the meter the wrong way round – which did not deter them from demanding money for reconnecting the supply. (Mr Sinclair is himself a Gas Board security man.) And in September 1984 Gas Board men broke into the house of Mrs Jayne Price, of Earlswood in Surrey, removing the meter and cutting her off. It was such a pity that they had chosen the wrong house. . . . Subsequently the local manager apologized, and sent Mrs Price a bunch of flowers. History does not relate what she did with them.

I must also mention Mr Paul Aldridge of Wombourne, near Wolverhampton, who detected a gas leak under his garage. The only way to cope with it was to dismantle the garage. He did so, and the leak was repaired. The West Midlands Gas Board then told him that the garage must not be rebuilt, because the Board has right to access to underground pipes. A Gas Board official said: 'We could not allow the garage to be rebuilt on its original site.'

Mind you, Gas Boards are not unique. For instance, Mr Philip Barnard of Milton Keynes was astounded to receive a bill for £1,250,000 from the Anglian Water Authority. After protests, the Authority amended the bill to a mere £30,000. Mrs Barnard commented: 'I know my husband is a plumber, but I don't believe even he could have wasted that much water.' It transpired that the Barnards had received the bill for the whole of Milton Keynes!

British Rail, too, maintains equally high standards. In May 1985 a train stopped at Hamble, near Southampton, and the guard told the two would-be passengers: 'We've only made the stop to tell you we don't stop here on Sundays.' There is also the service from Blake Street, in the West Midlands, which takes the form of a fourteen-mile round trip to Lichfield and back. The journey is 'officially uneconomic', so that nobody is allowed to use it.

Of course, Twitmarshes continue to flourish in all official bodies. The Potato Marketing Board now hires private aircraft to fly over the land, photographing fields to make sure that farmers are not growing too many potatoes (in the future, no doubt, they will also use artificial satellites). Even the Armed Services are not exempt. In 1984 the Royal Navy issued a directive to the effect that no more paperclips were to be bought for the moment, to cut costs. One RN lieutenant was heretical enough to wonder how many paperclips it would take to equal the cost of one Trident missile.

Artistic Twitmarshes remain supreme. The Arts Council's 1984 exhibition at the Serpentine Gallery was of special interest. One exhibit, a sculpture by Richard Wentworth, consisted of what was described in a newspaper report as looking like a curled-back sardine tin floating on a round of steel on top of a washtub; it was intended to represent the sinking of the Argentine warship *General Belgrano*. Meanwhile, the Tate Gallery paid just over £1,000,000 for Giorgio de Chirico's masterpiece *The Uncertainty of the Poet*, showing a headless Venus de Milo together with several bunches of bananas.

There have been some interesting legal cases. Mr Brian Gardiner of Middlesbrough found an Alsatian with a broken leg and took it to the People's Dispensary for Sick Animals. As he waited in the queue, the Alsatian performed what is termed an indiscretion on the pavement. A dog warden pounced. Mr Gardiner was fined £5 for allowing the Alsatian to act as it did. He refused to pay, on the grounds that he was merely doing a good turn and it wasn't his Alsatian anyway. He was duly brought up before Teesside magistrates, and Mr Eddie Sheldon sentenced him to five days' imprisonment. Actually he was released after only one day because an anonymous wellwisher paid the fine, but Mr Sheldon was adamant, and said, 'We were dealing only with the man's wilful refusal to pay a fine.'

Equally heinous was the conduct of Mr Michael Elderfield. He was prosecuted in Cornwall for picking five daffodils which grew by the roadside; he assumed them to be wild, and Mother's Day was looming.

Police took immediate action. Mr Elderfield made a total of three court appearances before the magistrates threw out the charge; the total cost to the ratepayers came to more than £400.

The GPO continues to improve its efficiency. In 1985 the Post Office at Taunton sent out Christmas cards to all its major customers. Unfortunately they forgot to stamp the cards, and each recipient had to pay a surcharge upon delivery.

But various newspaper reports, plus Mr Tomlinson's letter, set me thinking. What about local councils? You will have to take my word for it that every case given in this book is based upon reports which I have no reason to believe are unreliable. I have altered no names, and twisted no facts. You may well find some of them incredible – but after all, this is 1985! Pearls of wisdom fall regularly from the lips of sages such as Mr Ken Livingstone, Mr Arthur Scargill and the Bishop of Durham. Long may they prosper; the world would be poorer without them, though in some cases the ratepayers would possibly be a good deal richer.

2

A Look Around

When discussing local councils and other official bodies, one has to get used to the jargon. For example, an old coot* is known as a 'senior citizen'; anyone who stands even remotely to the right of the political centre is a 'fascist', while a 'racist' is anyone who believes that the English are best. One soon gets used to it.

The main areas in which Twitmarshes seem to be well to the fore are (1) expenditure, (2) race and (3) sex. I suppose that the most famous example of all might be that of the Salisbury Ski-Jump. A development company submitted plans for a multistorey car park near the city centre. Once these had been approved, the helpful council built an elevated road, curving high above ground level and suitably out of harm's way so that it would connect with the top of the car park. Unfortunately the developers then changed their minds, and the park was never built – but the road remained for twelve long years, ending forlornly in mid-air. Finally it was dismantled, though traces of it remain as a historic landmark. I once recommended that it might be used as a satellite launching rack, but for some reason or other my suggestion was not taken up.

* Like me. R.T.F.

The cost of town twinning can also be quite high. It is reported that Lambeth Council, led by Mr Ted Knight, has been twinned with one town in Russia, two in Germany, one in France, one in Nicaragua, and two striking Kent miners' villages – it was said that the cost was about £1000 a time, though this may well be an overestimate.

I particularly like the leaflet circulated by Manchester City Council with the aim of helping ratepayers to claim their housing benefits. It ends: 'Please note that your rate or rent rebate cannot be more than your rates or rent.' And in Torbay, the council proposed to appoint a warden to follow dirty dogs and stick little red flags into their droppings – to warn passers-by of their presence. I have not been able to find out whether this suggestion was actually implemented.

Foreign travel can have its moments of unbudgeted expense, too. According to a newspaper report in early 1984, four parish councillors from Whitehill, in Hampshire, visited their French twin town, Condé-sur-Vire in Normandy. Wine flowed freely, and at a late hour the Whitehill deputation suggested that their hosts should pay a return visit, bringing their football team over for a friendly match. This was subsequently forgotton – until the French football team duly turned up at Whitehill. Entertaining them cost the ratepayers more than £1000. The outcome of the football match does not seem to be on record.

Animals are not neglected. Have you heard of SNIP – the Society for Neutering Islington Pussies? Apparently it really exists. And in November 1984 it was announced that the Islington Council was to finance a birth control campaign for operations on dogs – or rather bitches only (a scheme which might well be condemned as sexist). The estimated cost was around £3000, though again I am not sure whether it was actually put into effect.

Ipswich was in the news again in May 1984, when a new swimming-pool complex was opened. The total cost was £5,800,000, helped by a £200,000 grant from the Suffolk County Council. At a cost of £11,000, a

Clacton company was employed to import coconut palms, pineapple bushes and banana plants to make the whole thing look exotic. I'm sure it did! And so did Flansham Park in Sussex. In the autumn of 1983, flowers were planted there by order of the Arun Council. In the following March, the same council ordered that the flowers should be cut down.

To round off this introduction, I feel I must mention two more news items. Mr Rod Humby has become Britain's first official Batman; he is being paid to watch over bats hanging about in church towers in Wales. And in 1984 the Blackburn District Council decided to give £300 to the Campaign for Freedom of Information, a group designed to combat secrecy in public places. The decision was taken by the grants sub-committee – in secret.

Let us now turn to more specific cases.

3

Support the Good Cause!

The GLC (Greater London Council) is, of course, noted for its support for thoroughly deserving causes. Using ratepayers' money, it has an impressive list. In the following collection, three are not genuine (I added them myself) and the rest are. I suggest, discerning reader, that you read through the list and then pick out the three fakes. If you succeed, you will be fully entitled to a cigar, but don't cheat and look at the answers on Page 90 before you have made up your mind!

1 Chinese Information and Advice Centre
2 Babies Against the Bomb
3 Chilean Cultural Committee
4 Sensible Footwear (Performing Arts)
5 Irish Video Project
6 Association of Burmese Musicians
7 Pakistan Welfare Society
8 Lesbian Feminist Writers Conference Planning Group
9 Only Women Press
10 Union of Turkish Workers
11 Gay Police Watch
12 London Gay Teenage Group
13 Welsh Harp Conservation Group
14 Londoners Against Radioactive Materials

15 Gaelic Liberation Group
16 Academy of Indian Dance
17 Black Theatre Cooperative
18 National Committee for Racism in Children's Books
19 Federation of Spanish Migrant Workers
20 Black Productions for African National Congress
21 Association of Brazilian Artists
22 Lesbian Line
23 *Spare Rib*

24 Commission of Filipino Migrant Workers
25 Bangladesh Women's Association
26 El Salvador Women's Committee
27 *Black on Black* Magazine
28 London Wall Ltd (Women's Mural Project)
29 Art of the Puppet Limited
30 Greater London Lesbian and Gay Employment Campaign
31 First International Feminist Book Fair Group
32 Black Female Prisoners' Scheme
33 Women and the Law Video Collective
34 Extemporary Dance Theatre
35 Association of Jamaicans UK Trust
36 Latin American Advisory Committee
37 Conference of Ethnic Minority Senior Citizens
38 Caribbean Slide Project
39 Women's Reproductive Right
40 Cypriot Youth Against Pit Closures

Do your best!

4

The Golliwog's Cake-Walk

Racial prejudice has been described as a pigment of the imagination. This isn't a very good pun and it isn't really true, because it implies that one race is superior to another – whichever way round it works. And we must admit that some of the statements and comments about it all are a little extreme. For instance, according to a working party set up in 1984 by the ILEA, *all* white people are racist, because they alone benefit from discrimination against black people. (It was notable that in this document, said to provide guidelines for 'multi-education in the Youth Service', the word *white* appeared with a lower-case w, while *Black* always had a capital B. But perhaps this was due simply to a shortage of capital Ws at the printing works.) In my last book I made the casual suggestion that chess is a racist game, as it sets blacks against whites, and that it would be only right to redesign the pieces, making them – say – violet and gamboge. The reply was somewhat guarded, but largely in agreement. I could also have pointed out that chess is sexist, because the key figure in the whole game is the king.

But was Debussy a racist composer? Frankly it would not have occurred to me, but it might have done to the councils of Birmingham, Lewisham and Islington had they chanced to hear *The Golliwog's*

Cake-Walk. Golliwogs are purely racist, and an energetic campaign against them was launched during 1984 and 1985.

It seems to have started in Islington, where the famous symbol of Robertson's jams and marmalades was included in a road safety exhibition. Posters headed 'Golly's Cycling Sense' gave tips to children about road safety, and formed part of a display supported by the Department of the Environment and the Royal Society for the Prevention of Accidents. Horrors! It was spotted, and removed, by Councillor Barbara Rogers, who was reported as saying, 'The golly is an offensive caricature of a black man and is undoubtedly regarded as being racist.' The GLC agreed, and said that no more products would be bought from Robertson's. The Birmingham Council outlawed golliwogs and then the gollies caused an even greater stir at the fairytale Jam Garden in Liverpool's International Garden Festival. Councillors demanded that they should be removed at once.

Not to be outdone, the Lewisham Borough Council agreed to spend £5600 on a report and film about 'the psychological effects of golliwogs', in order to 'raise the consciousness of black people in Lewisham'. And back in Islington, Mrs Gill Wing, who keeps a shop, came under heavy fire for selling golliwog novelties. The Labour Council's Anti-Racist Working Party, headed by Councillor Derek Hines, was reported as writing firmly to her, suggesting that the gollies should be withdrawn. Mrs Wing was not impressed, and, piquantly, the sale of gollies rocketed. 'We've had an absolutely fantastic response,' said Mrs Wing. 'Orders for golliwogs have poured in. We're selling more than ever, both by post and in the shop.' Golly toys, teapots and toast-racks became, briefly, all the rage.

Apparently Mr Hines was upset, and a newspaper reported his comment: 'Unfortunately, it got blown up by the Press into something completely different, and this was used to mock this Labour Council.' Mock the Labour Council? Perish the thought!

Robertson's were not alone. In order to check on racist firms, the GLC sent out a questionnaire to all those firms with which they had dealings. All firms had to give details about their employment of ethnic minorities and women. Rowntrees, manufacturers of the famous Kit-Kat chocolate, demurred. Their reply was polite, but in essence it indicated that Mr Ken Livingstone and his colleagues on the GLC could stuff their forms. The staff committee chairman, Mr John Carr, was reported as saying, 'We are very concerned that ratepayers' and taxpayers' money does not go to subsidize racial and sex discrimination.' So Kit-Kat joined the Robertson golliwog in the limbo of outlawed things.

So great care must always be taken not to offend anyone. There was a particularly blatant case in Islington recently, where Ms Irene Piedger, a council clerk, was disciplined by the council for failing to make sure that a black colleague, Ms Linda Braithwaite, was coming to the Christmas lunch! Ms Piedger was instructed to attend a 'racism awareness course' run by the council, and warned that any future offence of the same kind would result in dismissal. I quote from the *Daily Mail* report on the case, on 19 May: 'Irene – who was summoned to the court with four housing clerks – has been effectively silenced until her appeal. Officials at the Town Hall – where the next Lady Mayoress is to be a homosexual man – have threatened her with instant dismissal if she talks about the case. But Irene said: 'We asked Linda face to face if she wanted to come to the party. She didn't get back to us, so we assumed she wasn't interested. I didn't have a chance to say a word at the kangaroo court. Since the complaint, she's been promoted from Grade 3 to Grade 4.' Ms Piedger had no idea just what a racial awareness course was. However, Islington's Mayor, Ms Marjorie Ogilvy, who chaired the disciplinary hearing, was quoted as saying, 'This was the lightest penalty we could give.'

Obviously, such lapses must be avoided in future. May I suggest that a small notebook be carried around, to be consulted each morning:

1 Ask Ms P. whether she has remembered to make an appointment with her dentist.
2 Inquire after Mr Q.'s bunion.
3 See whether Ms R. plans to attend the Multi-Racial Coffee Morning on Tuesday.
4 Check on Ms S.'s availability for the outing to Aldgate East on 6 January.

This might provide a reasonable safeguard against further compulsory attendance at a racial awareness course.

The funny thing about race relations is that in many cases it seems to work in one direction only. For instance, not long ago newspapers printed some acid comments about GLC posters which, it was said, were produced under the direction of Mr Ken Livingstone. One showed a black person trapped in a burning room and whites ignoring his plight by covering their eyes, ears or mouths with their hands. Another showed a group of people, all white, hiding what were called 'the tools of their trade', such a a policeman's truncheon. A petition from some workers in Brent's Chalkhill district housing office made the dangerously pointless speculation that if the roles of black and white people in the posters had been reversed, there would have been 'frightening repercussions'.

Advertisements have also been criticized. Thus Lambeth Council in April 1985: 'The post of Welfare Rights Officer (Ethnic Minorities) is seen as being a post which can only be filled by a member of the black community, and the provisions of Section 52 (d) of the Race Relations Act will be applied. Therefore, only members of the black community will be considered for this post.'

Hackney Council did its best in 1984. It was reported in April that £327,000 had been spent during the last financial year advertizing posts in small-circulation ethnic newspapers, including £26,000 to a Punjabi language newspaper which failed to produce a single applicant. In Hackney, indeed, it was said that all applicants for jobs with the borough were being vetted by a special Race Relations Office. The race vetters

LAMBETH B.C.
APPLICANTS
FOR THE POST OF
WELFARE RIGHTS
OFFICER
(ETHNIC MINORITIES)
PLEASE SIT HERE
AND WAIT YOUR
TURN.
MILLWALL
LOVE
HATE

included a West Indian on the short list for a £13,000-a-year post as Community Arts Officer, though he had originally been turned down because of insufficient qualifications.

A similar attitude was evident in Westminster North. The local Labour Party there wanted only women, ethnic minorities and manual workers to be nominated as candidates at the next General Election.

There are, however, occasional exceptions to the overall pattern. In 1985 the Women's Reproductive Rights Information Centre, which receives a £50,000 annual grant from the GLC, advertized for a part-time advice worker. Miss Lorrien Finlay applied. She was not shortlisted, because, as the council frankly said, she was white, and it had been 'decided to shortlist women of ethnic origin only'. Miss Finlay was incensed enough to take the matter to court, and was awarded £250 damages, though lawyer Ms Ros Alexander, for the women's group, was reported in the newspapers as saying that although the Race Relations Act had been contravened, Miss Finlay wouldn't have got the job anyway.

Remember that racial education cannot begin too early. In November 1984 the GLC was reported as approving a £95,366 grant to an eight-strong group, seven of them women, entitled the Lewisham Mobile Crèche Project, whose aim was to provide 'good quality anti-racist and anti-sexist play activities for the under-fives', or in some cases the under-threes. The grant was to go toward financing, among other things, a van and equipment, playmats, a climbing frame, various toys, and rattles.

5

What's in a Name?

Local councils are often quite firm about names. In particular, some long-established names have been rejected as being totally out of touch with modern thinking. For example, there was the question of Rhodesia Road in North Lambeth. The Lambeth Council's Joint Urgency Sub-Committee duly met, and issued a Press release as part of its Anti-Racist Year. In view of the impending visit to England of the South African Prime Minister, and the fact that the racist régime in Rhodesia had been replaced by the enlightened rule of Mr Mugabe, it was decided to rename Rhodesia Road as Zimbabwe Road.

This was an important decision, and it opens the way for an extensive programme of renaming. Perhaps my own suggestions might be considered for the near future?

Old name	*Suggested new name (R.T.F.)*
Salisbury Cathedral	Harare People's Church
King's Cross	Commissar's Cross
Horse Guards Parade	CND Avenue
Nelson's Column	Scargill Monument
Prince Consort Road	Supreme Soviet Road
Eton College	Berkshire Comprehensive School
Victoria Station	Stalin Station

Old name	*Suggested new name (R.T.F.)*
Whitehall	Multiracial Hall
Blackfriars Bridge	Caribbean Brothers' Bridge
Heathrow Airport	Livingstonerow Airport
Green Park	Red Park
Oxford Circus	Oxford People's Theatre
Commercial Road	Cooperative Road
Manchester	Personchester

I can't think what to do about Barons Court, Earls Court, and Queensway!

Another intriguing idea was proposed at about the same time by Camden Council. This was to honour black heroes, such as Nelson Mandela and Martin Luther King, by naming dustcarts after them. The Works Department Officer, Mr Peter Swingler, was quoted as adding, 'We could give names to our larger vehicles. They could be painted – or we could use plaques, like those on railway engines.'

6
Red Peter

Children are particularly prone to racial prejudice. I have already referred to the case of chess, though one has to be doubly careful here. Black and white must go, of course, but other colours should also be avoided; blue would be pro-Tory and therefore political, while yellow would clearly be an insult to the Chinese.

So far as literature is concerned, the trend seems to have been set originally not in Britain, but in America, where a Mr Douglas Larche of Iowa published a revised edition of nursery rhymes. 'Little Boy Blue' was turned into 'Little Girl Green', while 'Mary Had a Little Lamb' was turned into 'Bobby Had a Baby Goat' – though in order not to offend vegetarians, I would prefer 'Mary Had a Little Nut-Cutlet'. Mr Larche complained that many rhymes were sexist or racist. 'The implications are clear,' he said. 'Girls may be flower-tenders, frightened curd-eaters, seamstresses and imprisoned pumpkin-shell residents, while boys are kings, masters and candlestick-jumpers.'

The idea spread rapidly to our own fair land. How about 'Three Blind Mice'? The Teachers for Animal Rights Organization is vocal here. The campaign's organizer was reported as saying that the rhyme should be banned from schools because it ridicules and degrades animals. She added, 'Women, black people

And the Snowperson took Kay away to the Ice Palace.
HANS ALLFAITH ANDERCHILD FAIRY TALES

and animals are living beings and should not have to suffer fear, harassment, injustice, ridicule and the deprivation of basic rights.' She also condemned violence toward animals through milk drinking, zoo trips and so on. And Mr Tam Dixon of the Birmingham Council was quoted as objecting to sexist pictures, such as those showing John helping Dad with the car while Janet stayed with Mum in the kitchen.

One of the worst examples of all, according to the Lambeth Council, is that of Tufty Fluffytail, the Road Safety character who was made popular by the Royal Society for the Prevention of Accidents (RoSPA). The Lambeth Council's safety committee regarded Tufty as both racist and sexist, with white middle-class bias. A senior council official explained, 'The voices used on films of the characters are standard English. They say things like 'jolly' and 'super' – that's not what kids in Lambeth say,' and the whole Tufty road show shows a 'lack of awareness of the multiracial and multicultural nature of society'.

I suppose it isn't really Tufty's fault that modern Lambeth children tend to say 'xxxx!' and 'xxxxxx!' instead of 'jolly' and 'super'. Mr Peter Davis, Lambeth's Tory opposition leader, did comment that 'I suppose Tufty would be approved of if he were gay and black instead of brown and furry. They must be going nuts.' But Lambeth Council was unimpressed. Talks were to be held with RoSPA, and Mr Trevor Davies, consumer services officer, said that 'if agreement cannot be reached, we would necessarily have to avoid the use of Tufty characters'.

Poor little squirrel!

Children's jokes are equally at fault. The ILEA Equal Opportunities Unit recently ordered all its schools to be on the lookout for the Unigate Dairy's Joke Book, which was quite shockingly racist and sexist. Imagine it! There was even a joke about a cannibal who was vegetarian – he only ate Swedes. This almost warrants a strong protest to Westminster from the Stockholm Government. The ILEA was most concerned, and said that it 'feared children might bring the books into schools', so that a grave warning was printed in the ILEA newspaper *Contact*. Note also that the Islington Council has employed two people to search for Irish jokes, and ruthlessly stamp them out.*

Enid Blyton's books are equally racist in view of the fact that in her Toyland, golliwogs are so often depicted as villains – at least, so opined the Race Relations Liaison Committee of the Liverpool Council in June 1984. Titles of other books such as *Ten Little Niggers* and *Little Black Sambo* had, of course, long since been outlawed. (Did you realize that W.S. Gilbert's libretto in *The Mikado* had been censored long ago? In *The Mikado's* opening song, 'blacked like a nigger' has been turned into 'painted with vigour'. I have a feeling that Gilbert himself would have been highly entertained.) It was reported, too, that Liverpool education officials were now 'examining scores of titles used in the city's nursery, primary and secondary schools

* Have you heard the one about the Irish firing squad? They stood in a circle.

before deciding if any more stories should be outlawed'.

The campaign has recently spread to New Zealand, where the country's Race Relations Board complained about no less a person than Dr Dolittle, created by Hugh Lofting many years ago. In one book, a black prince stated categorically that he wanted to be white.

In the ILEA, Ms Frances Morrell is, rightly, concerned with eradicating all racist, sexist and 'classist' books from children's education. Consider Robinson Crusoe, who is obviously imperialist; Tom Sawyer and Jane Eyre who are equally clearly sexist, and all the Ladybird books are inadmissible because – as was pointed out in Birmingham – boys help in the garage and girls don't. Further warnings were issued by the ILEA about Shakespeare and Dickens. *King Lear* is a sexist play, while *Oliver Twist* is blatantly anti-Semitic. And what on earth can be said in defence of Beatrix Potter's middle-class rabbits?

Next, a detailed report which appeared in the *Sunday Telegraph* for 31 March 1985. According to this a Church primary school in North Kensington received a visit in 1983 from an ILEA inspector, Ms Pamela Pullen, and the library was carefully checked. Out went *The Adventures of Tom Sawyer*, *Jane Eyre* and others, plus the Tin-tin books, which were imperialist and anti-conservationist and did not show women in an advantageous light. The headmaster was reprimanded about the dangerous middle-class bias of the children's books; the school library was closed down, and all the Ladybird books were ordered to be destroyed. In fact, the headmaster gave them away to parents at 5p a time, though even here he had misgivings that the ILEA would object to his polluting the parents with sexist, racist and middle-class propaganda. The report added that he was so demoralized by the turn of events that he left abruptly to take up a quiet job as a church archivist.

There was a curious sequel. The ILEA wrote to the newspaper saying that the report was highly misleading, but the writer of the article was unabashed. I can make no personal comment. I wrote to Ms Pullen to see whether I could get hold of the full story. No reply!

And now we come to perhaps the most flagrant case of all – that of the children's BBC TV programme, 'Blue Peter' (which has, incidentally, raised huge sums of money for charity).

Mr Robert Ferguson, the £17,000-a-year head of media studies at London University's Institute of Education, voiced his opinions in *TV and Schooling*, a collection of essays on published by the British Film Institute's Education Department. 'Blue Peter', he was quoted as saying, showed a limited 'universe of discourse' which was 'Anglo-centric, ostensibly Christian and tends to argue that the best way of dealing with social problems is through benevolence'. He would like to replace it with a programme of the same format, but to be presented by two women and one man; it would be 'openly anti-royalist, anti-racist and anti-sexist, and it would deplore the need for charity when millions of pounds are spent each minute on defence'.

Well, 'Red Peter' would certainly be an innovation. . .

7

Queerer and Queerer

There was a time, in the dim past, when homosexuality was regarded as a Bad Thing, and was punished by imprisonment or worse. As the years passed by, more enlightened thinking prevailed, so that homosexuals became 'queers' and were tolerated. Next they became 'gays', and were sometimes lauded.

This was highlighted in 1984, when the women's committee of the Brent Council was incensed at posters advertizing Thursday afternoon tea dances and Saturday night dances at their Town Hall – the posters actually showed *men dancing with women*! As Councillor Angela Shariff told a meeting of the council, according to a newspaper report, 'Not everybody is a married couple. There are gay people and lesbians in this borough, and the publicity should reflect that accurately.' In future, therefore, it was only right for posters to show men dancing with other men, and women with other women.

Further enlightened legislation was in the pipeline. Councillors at Greenwich called for lessons on homosexuality to be given in schools. In Lewisham a report said that women running a baby unit could not qualify for a £45,000 grant unless they involved lesbians, while some months earlier Haringey Council was said to be trying to recruit gay play-leaders; it was

also suggested that the wearing of wedding rings was embarrassing for gays in general. There was also a report by the council's Community Afairs Committee which recommended teaching children about homosexual heroes in history. 'The suppression of lesbian and gay issues in the school curriculum,' read the report, 'robs pupils, and other teachers, of important historical, cultural and literary content. . . . Gay or lesbian teachers should be able to talk about their sexuality in exactly the same way that heterosexual teachers already do.' It was also recommended that Haringey lesbians and gays would benefit from a special centre, a record library and a special advice bureau.

Now and then there are unreasonable reactionary protests. For instance when the Rugby Council announced that it would not, in future, employ any but heterosexuals, there were immediate repercussions. Mr Jeffrey Coupe, a Labour councillor, condemned this 'irresponsible motion', while Mr John Daly, of Nalgo, warned that there would be a national protest inasmuch as the Rugby Council had displayed a total lack of understanding.

Islington Council has always been in the forefront of progress, quite apart from the now legendary provision of wrestling mats for lesbians and the idea of cemeteries for women only. A grant of £3000 was made for the special benefit of Irish lesbians, who had come to the borough to 'escape conservative attitudes and repressive legislation'. And there was a real breakthrough in the spring of 1985, with the appointment of the new deputy mayor of the borough with his deputy mayoress. I quote from the *Mail* report of 18 May, 'Mr Bob Crossman, a councillor who is openly homosexual, poses happily with his official consort, Martin McCloghry, both of them wearing their chains of office. . . If Labour retains control in the Borough, they will be 'mayor' and 'mayoress' next year. Mr Crossman is chairman of a lesbian and gay sub-committee, and is apparently regarding his job as deputy mayor as an advance for homosexuals. "As far as I know I'll be the first gay mayor in London," he said. He and Mr McCloghry, who lives with him, are already carrying out civic duties together in the borough, which has been redubbed the Socialist Republic of Islington.'

To conclude, let us note the deplorable action of the government in holding up a grant of £100,000 to the London Lesbian and Gay Centre, which had been set up in a five-storey building near Smithfield market bought by the GLC for £300,000, and had been officially opened by Councillors Andy Harris and Valerie Wise. Let us hope that the government reconsiders.

8

Postman Pat in the Doghouse

Do you remember Postman Pat? He putt-putts around, on the television screen and in books, in his tiny Royal Mail van, Pat 1. Now, sadly, he must go – so says that monument of wisdom, the ILEA. After eighteen teachers had spent two years in an exhaustive campaign of investigation, it has been disclosed that Postman Pat is rabidly sexist.

Why? Because he is a Post*man*. And the term 'man' is hopelessly out of touch with modern thinking in a world where women have, surely, an equal claim to priority. There are other similar examples. For instance, the ILEA committee also insisted that Father should not automatically be assumed to be the head of the household, and there are many other cases of sexist terms which must be weeded out. Indeed, a list was drawn up by that august body, the National Union of Journalists. Once again I give you a list of examples. Try to pick out two false entries – and as before, don't cheat by looking first at the answers on page 90. Here is the list:

Instead of:	*Use:*
1 Businessman	Business manager, head of firm, etc
2 Cameraman	Photographer, camera operator

Instead of:	*Use:*
3 Dustman	Refuse collector
4 Chairman	Chairperson
5 Woman doctor	Doctor
6 Man in the street	Average citizen, average voter
7 Man or mankind	Humanity, human race, humans
8 Manmade	Synthetic, artificial, manufactured*
9 Ice-cream man	Ice-cream seller
10 Authoress	Author
11 Manhood	Adulthood
12 Foreman	Supervisor
13 Newsman	Journalist, reporter
14 Girls (over 18)	Women
15 Ford men voted. . .	Ford workers voted . . .
16 Male nurse	Nurse
17 Steward	Airline staff, flight attendant
18 Fireman	Firefighter
19 Manning	Staffing
20 Policeman	Police officer

Did you pick out the fake entries? Now look. Incidentally, Mrs and Miss should be avoided like Bubonic plague. Always use Ms.

Mr Mike Cliss, an engineer with Avon Council's housing department in Bristol, faced big trouble in December 1984. As secretary of the Town Hall union's

* But should not this be 'personufactured'? The NUJ seems to have slipped up here.

sports club he forgot himself and referred to 'ladies' netball'. Consternation! Mr Steve Lamprey, the branch vice-chairman, wrote strongly to Mr Cliss, stating that a complaint from a woman member had been received about this sexist language. Mr Lamprey went on, 'The committee agreed with the complaint made, and several members referred to similar complaints at their workplace from women members.' To everyone's surprise, Mr Cliss resigned.

Christmas is traditionally the season of forgiveness and goodwill, but beware of pantomimes – at least if you live in Lewisham. There, a production of *Jack and the Beanstalk* was found to include both racist and sexist propaganda. A spokesperson for the Lewisham Council referred to discussions between the entertainment staff and the producer, Mr Paul Elliott, as 'last year our panto had some areas which were sexist and racist and we had complaints'. Council officials sat solemnly through rehearsals. Out went a joke about the GLC leader, Mr Ken Livingstone, and in went a joke about Mr Norman Tebbit. Out went the line 'a nice kind gentleman', to be replaced by 'a nice kind person'. Out went the King's announcement to Jack, 'Whoever slays the giant wins for his bride my daughter', as the term 'win' was condemned as sexist. I have not been able to find out what was inserted instead.

To my mind, the most revolutionary proposal of all has come from a Women's Forum made up of local councillors and officials from female organizations in the West Midlands. It was put forward in January 1985 by Ms Rosa Dangerfield, who suggested that there

should be a night curfew for all men throughout Britain. Originally it seems that Ms Dangerfield was being somewhat flippant, but then she altered her mind. 'I thought hard about it,' she was reported as saying, 'and now I think that I made a good suggestion. Respectable women are too scared to go out at night, and that is wrong. If men were barred from the streets after darkness we could get rid of the problems.' Thoughtfully, though, she added, 'Obviously, some men have to be out after dark. Those with genuine business could be issued with special permits.' The Women's Committee took the idea very seriously, and it was supported by the chairperson.

Mind you, there are just a few snags – and didn't W.S. Gilbert have roughly the same idea in *Princess Ida*, where in Castle Adamant everything male was banned, and at dawn what sounded like the crowing of a cockerel was actually carried out by 'an accomplished hen'? So perhaps some of us may be forgiven for regarding the whole sexist campaign as a load of horse-personure!

9

The Freedom of the Press

Early in 1985 a complaint against the *Daily Express*, *Daily Mail* and *Standard* was upheld by the Press Council. It concerned a seventeen-year-old youth who had appeared in court and been found guilty of a rather nasty crime. The complaint, by a Mr R. Borzello of North London, complained that the papers had described the youth as 'black, slightly built'. The Press Council agreed that it was wrong to describe him as black, since this was 'irrelevant and should not have been introduced into the reports'.

The point is well taken, and I feel that it could be considerably extended. For example, let us consider the following case, which is, I must stress, entirely fictitious.

Miss Lucy Jones, a black housewife living in Sussex, appeared in court on a charge of misappropriating the sum of £3 belonging to Major T. Pott, late of the Indian Army, during an excursion of the Bognor Regis Birdwatching Society to Pagham Harbour. Miss Jones, who is aged thirty-four, explained that the apparent discrepancy in the society's funds was due to a misunderstanding, and the case was dismissed.

Now let us see what deletions should be made.

1 MISS Jones. This is sexist, because it implies that the lady concerned was unmarried and thus at a disadvantage compared with a married woman. Delete.
2 BLACK housewife. As the Press Council has explained, this is irrelevant. Delete.
3 HOUSEWIFE. This is a thoroughly sexist and derogatory term. Delete.

We now have:

Lucy Jones, living in Sussex, appeared in court on a charge of misappropriating the sum of £3 belonging to Major T. Pott, late of the Indian Army, during an excursion of the Bognor Regis Birdwatching Society to

Pagham Harbour. Jones, who is aged thirty-four, explained that the apparent discrepancy in the society's funds was due to a misunderstanding, and the case was dismissed.

Now let us take matters further.

4 LIVING IN SUSSEX. This is irrelevant, and unfair to Sussex residents, most of whom are thoroughly worthy and law-abiding. Delete.
5 MAJOR T. Pott. The military rank has no bearing on the case, and is imperialist. Delete.
6 AGED THIRTY-FOUR. Again irrelevant, and it is sexist to give an age in such a case. Delete.

We now have:

Lucy Jones appeared in court on a charge of misappropriating the sum of £3 belonging to T. Pott, during an excursion of the Bognor Regis Birdwatching Society to Pagham Harbour. Jones explained that the apparent discrepancy in the society's finds was due to a misunderstanding, and the case was dismissed.

But we haven't finished yet.

7 BOGNOR REGIS BIRDWATCHING SOCIETY. Mention of the society's name casts unfair aspersions on the society itself. Delete.
8 APPEARED IN COURT. This infers potential guilt, and is unfair. Delete.

9 THE SUM OF £3. In view of the smallness of the sum concerned, the case is so obviously minor that it is unfair to give details. Delete.

So we have:

Lucy Jones appeared concerning a sum due to T. Pott. Jones explained that the apparent discrepancy was due to a misunderstanding, and the case was dismissed.

But all in all, the fact that the case was dismissed is proof that it should never have been brought, and any report is therefore unfair to the defendant. This means that according to official ruling, the entire report should be deleted.

Of course, it follows that if the rules are rigidly applied, all daily newspapers will be issued as a set of virtually blank pages. But, after all, isn't it always said that no news is good news?

10

Please, Teacher . . .

A stirring pronouncement was made early in 1985 by the ILEA. Eleven-a-side football, it was said, should be kicked out of primary schools as being both exclusive and sexist. Ms Iris Tappenden, a London headmistress, was quoted as saying that 'Football is a violent, aggressive sport. It is very selective and excludes many children . . . . ' Two schools, Downderry and Launcelot in Lewisham, at once agreed to pull out of the Lewisham Schools League in South London. Elsewhere, matches and training sessions were relegated to after-school hours.

In a BBC interview an ILEA official explained that football was frowned upon because girls did not have a fair chance.* Of course, it is quite true that boys are not similarly handicapped, because they can take part in activities traditionally confined to girls, and this

* I am a mere cricketer, and so I am indebted to a friend of mine for the following information. Whatever the ILEA may say about opening football to both sexes, the Football Association has full control over the game and will not allow football to be played by mixed sexes, as it is considered too dangerous for any females who might take part. However, they do allow females to referee men's football matches, though at times referees do get thumped by irate players. My friend says that he has not, however, heard of a female referee being assaulted.

gives rise to a possible conversation, which is entirely of my own construction (R.T.F.) but may perhaps be not entirely irrelevant:

Scene: The parlour of a house in South London. *Characters:* Father (aged thirty) and Johnny (aged nine).

JOHNNY	But please, I want to play football with the boys!
FATHER	It's not good for you, son. It's sexist and exclusive.
JOHNNY	Please, what does 'exclusive' mean? (*There is a baffled silence.*)
FATHER	Never you mind, son. Just listen to me.
JOHNNY	But what can I do if I'm not going to play football?
FATHER	Well, why not join in with all the others? There's a Peace Study class, for example.
JOHNNY	But last time we had a Peace Study class, everyone ended up fighting!
FATHER	Never mind, son. That's make you ready for football when you leave school. *Curtain.*

So far as CSE studies are concerned, a new subject was reportedly introduced at the Golden Hillock*

* Yes, Claude. The name is *Hill*ock.

School at Sparkbrook, Birmingham, the constituency of Mr Roy Hattersley. This dealt with the art of organizing protest demonstrations. As one project, it was reported in the newspapers that pupils marched on the head teacher's study waving placards and demanding better toilets, and that the headmistress, Ms Mary Stirling Stuart, was adamant that this was quite in order: 'We are teaching the ways in which the country

allows pupils to demonstrate. It has nothing to do with violence or riots.' Of course not! Such an idea is absurd. We must applaud Ms Sandra Schmidt, headmistress of the William Patten School in Stoke Newington, who was reported as giving left-wing lessons to her five-year-olds because of what she felt was her duty to counter 'right-wing bias'; it was also said that she led her school in a half-day walkout in support of striking miners and a staff demonstration against a police open day for children. Reassuringly, the ILEA inspectors agreed that they were 'satisfied that the work of the school on the 3Rs is of a good standard', so all is well. Meanwhile Ms Anne Percival, of King Edward VI Camp School for Girls in King's Heath, Birmingham, banned the school song because 'it smacks too much of Empire'. The chorus ran:

Forward where the knocks are hardest,
Some to failure, some to fame.
Never mind the cheers or hooting,
Keep your head and play the game.

Ms Percival commented that the song 'was written before the school had any coloured pupils', and was 'embarrassing in a multi-cultural society which we have today'. I quite agree. Are there any suggestions for a replacement chorus, I wonder?

Still on the musical front, some schools have already outlawed the works of Mozart and Beethoven as 'élitist'. At a conference in Chester, Mr Peter Maxwell Davies, President of the Schools Music Association, said that he had 'met young specialist music teachers who can hardly read music and consider the exclusive use of pop music as essential for holding the kids' attention'. There are racist songs, too. What about 'White Christmas'? The last line should surely be altered to 'Let all my Christmases be multi-racial'.

Some school textbooks leave a great deal to be desired. An ILEA report in December 1984 concerned geography, and was prepared by a group of eighteen teachers, ten women and eight men. It said that the emphasis at present was almost exclusively on the economic role of men, with most textbooks showing men sitting on tractors and taking all the decisions, while women adopted domestic or passive roles. It would therefore be more apt to show how women in Third World countries hoe the fields and collect water. (It was not, however, suggested that men should generally be shown working hard at their embroidery.)

Mathematical books are even worse. Not long ago Mr Europe Singh, of the ILEA anti-racist team, stated, according to reports, that 'It is naïve to argue that western mathematics teaching is politically neutral.' Many problems involve profit, loss and interest rates, and therefore have an ideological basis. Even the traditional subtraction method of borrowing and paying back uses terms that are 'mainly a reflection of the concerns of mercantile capitalism'. Much more logically, it has been said, children should be asked to work out the ratio of population to land among different racial groups in South Africa; reckon the probability of an African miner earning as much as a white workmate;

draw graphs illustrating unemployment among different ethnic groups in Britain, and calculate the percentage success rates of discrimination complaints to the Commission for Racial Equality.

Certainly these points are entirely valid, and perhaps I may be allowed to propose a couple of standard questions which might be included in a new textbook, if the ILEA would agree, of course. Try and work them out – answers on page 90.

1 In 1989, strikes accounted for the loss of 4675 working hours at a capitalist factory in East Grinstead. The total number of scabs not on strike was 53. If the work force amounts to 255 men and 623 women, and the loss to the factory amounts to £23.10p. per hour per striker, calculate the total loss to the capitalist management.

2 In the same firm, the management's original offer per year was an increase of 0.2 per cent. After successful industrial action this was increased to 48.2 per cent. If the former working wages was £289 for a 15-hour week, calculate the new weekly wage negotiated after justifiable industrial action.

The NUT (National Union of Teachers) is well in the picture. In 1984 it found a serious racist slur on a calendar issued to schools by the Defence Ministry. It showed Captain Nevill Maskelyne Smyth of the Queen's Bays winning the VC in the Sudan in 1898. Captain Smyth was white, and the Arab whom he was fighting was black. On the other hand, it is just possible that the NUT itself might have been criticized at the same time, as many teachers were on strike, and those who were not were condemned as 'blacklegs'. Shouldn't this be 'whitelegs'?

There are some highly progressive schools around. One was the Woodlands Residential School at Deganwy, North Wales, run by the Liverpool City Council. It was staffed by a host of teachers, cooks, cleaners and caretakers. Unfortunately, after being closed in June 1983, it had no pupils at all, and by March of the following year it was claimed that the cost to Liverpool ratepayers had been around £300,000. However, Mr Dominic Brady, Chairman of the Liverpool Education Committee, was quoted as explaining that the school would reopen, and one staff member stressed that the teachers attended daily meetings with the headmaster, Mr Owen. Morale, it was added, was 'quite high'.

Remedial education is not neglected, and one project of special worth was tried out by the Lewisham and Camden Councils. This involved sending thirteen 'problem teenagers' to a Danish-run progressive reform school on the Caribbean island of St Vincent. Among their activities was a trip to Venezuela, to 'broaden their outlook'. The estimated cost per pupil per week was in the region of £350, excluding air fares, naturally.

Alas, not everything went smoothly. Reports – whether accurate or not, I am in no position to say; certainly they were printed in the Press – alleged that among other activities were pot-smoking, glue-sniffing, violence and theft – including the theft of £5000 from the headmaster to buy drugs. (Mrs Vicky Ward, a North London youth centre director, and three of the parents were quoted in the *Daily Mail* for 28 April 1984 as supporting that particular comment.) A spokesperson for the Lewisham Council said, 'We gather some complaints have been made, but as the place is deliberately isolated it has been very difficult to get the exact picture.' Camden Council then dispatched two social workers to check on the situation. Mr Alan Woods, Chairman of the Camden Social Services Committee, was quoted as saying: 'I am convinced that this is a worthwhile project. We could seriously consider using it again.' But why the Caribbean or Venezuela? Why not, for example, the Seychelles or Hawaii? There must be plenty of choice.

Returning to entertainment, it is worth noting that in July 1984 some questions were asked about a play for schoolchildren put on at a youth theatre which receives a yearly £500,000 grant from the ILEA. The play, presented by the Rubber Jennies at the Marylebone Cockpit Theatre, had a mainly lesbian theme, and was described by a Labour spokesperson as a serious work about sex education; the scene was set against a blackcloth of giant birth-control-pill packets. Contrast this with the disgraceful BBC radio soap opera, 'The Archers'. When Mr Neil Kinnock, now Leader of the Labour Party, was Shadow Education Minister he wrote a 350-word letter to the producer, Mr Bill Smethurst. Mr Smethurst said that Mr Kinnock 'took great exception to the fact that one of our juvenile characters, Lucy Perks, passed the exam to get her into a grammar school. He clearly thought that Lucy should be going to a comprehensive school.'

Modern teachers are, of course, always properly trained. For instance, the newspapers recently carried a story that an applicant for a teaching post was rudely interrupted in the middle of explaining his athletic achievements by a questioner who wanted to know whether he had any GCEs to his name. How ridiculous! But examination results are often fascinating. One GCE teenage candidate in August 1984 seemed to have his history rather muddled, as he wrote: 'King Offer knocked orf the Danes. King Alfred knocked orf King Offer. Now we have Danish bacon.' But should we be ultra-critical? After all, there was the recent case of the written demand put forward by a group of striking teachers in pursuit of their claim for more money. It contained twenty spelling and grammar mistakes.

11

Without Comment

There are occasions when one has a feeling that the only thing to do is to give up. The following items seem to me to be more or less unclassifiable, and I merely give them as they have been reported in the Press.

In April 1985 the Stoke-on-Trent councillors began their meetings in a novel way. Sixty councillors got down on their knees and prayed to God to save their football team, Stoke City, from relegation to the Second Division. It was reported that the idea came from the Lord Mayor's chaplain, the Rev. Colin Crumpton, and was eagerly taken up by the Lord Mayor, Mr Jack Dimmock, who said, 'Every month before council meetings we pray for these in need, and Stoke City are very much in need right now.' A football club member confirmed that 'at the moment we need all the help we can get'.

Alas, God must have been hard-hearted. At the end of the season Stoke City were relegated, with more than twenty points less than the club immediately above them in the table.

Mr John Kent, who farms five acres at Tetbury in Gloucestershire, wanted to build a shed for a drake and four ducks. The shed would be about the size of a teachest. He was told that planning permission would be needed, and that failure to obtain this would result in the ducks being evicted. Mr Kent's plans were turned down. He then went to see Mr Len Cullimore, of the Cotswold District Council planning office in Cirencester, and met with the same answer. 'Normal planning considerations have been applied in Mr Kent's case,' it was said.

Quackers?

In February 1985 Mr Barry Burgess of Selsey, in Sussex, laid a gravel hard-standing on a piece of rough scrub ground outside his house, which had been covered with weeds and tree roots. It looked rather nice. However, the Chichester Council ordered him to remove it and restore the land to its status quo.

And when Victoria Road, Chichester, was resurfaced, it was dug up by the Gas Board within a week.

The Tyde Gate Inn on the Cambridgeshire–Lincolnshire border is in an odd situation. The county border runs right through the bar. At 2.30, the Cambridge end must be closed, but the Lincolnshire end can stay open until 5.30, so that customers have to move down the bar. There are two sets of policemen outside, two sets of licensing laws and two darts leagues.

In 1983 the Kensington and Chelsea Borough Committee decided to clean the bronze statues in Cheyne Walk, as they looked 'green and dirty'. They sandblasted them, removing the patina so that they

1.

2.

became a curious custard colour. Several thousands of pounds had to be spent in restoring an artificial patina, but at least it was said that at the end of the operation the statues 'looked cleaner'.

In St Helens, the Mayor will not be allowed to meet Rotarians, public school heads, and other 'free loaders and carpet baggers'. Mr Brian Green, leader of the St Helens Council, was reported as saying that 'the People's Mayor will have to identify with the struggles of the working class'.

Mr Conway, of Poplar Grove in Newcastle-under-Lyme, has had a curious situation to face. Poplar Grove is a small cul-de-sac. Mr Conway built a garage in his garden, but a year or two later the council built a large wall which made access to the garage difficult. Next there appeared a fence, which made access impossible. Mr E. Wetherell, the Borough Secretary, commented that a television programme about it all presented 'a very one-sided view of the situation' – but Mr Conway still can't get his car into his garage!

Mr and Mrs Taylor are beekeepers, living in Huntingdon, Cambridgeshire. They put up a small placard beside the road: *Visit Gray's Honey Shop, 500 yards.* Mr Pilling, the local planning officer for Huntingdon Council, ordered them to take it down, as it was an 'unduly prominent and incongruous feature to the visual amenities and existing rural character of the area'. It was, perhaps, a little unfortunate that the Honey Farm sign was not far from a much larger one, which said, in bold letters, SUPPORT YOUR COUNCIL LOTTERY AND HELP IMPROVE THESE AREAS.

In the *Daily Telegraph* for 28 December 1983, it was reported that claims for a £15 attendance allowance were made by some Labour members of the West Midlands County Council who went to hear Mr Neil Kinnock during his campaign for the Party leadership. Councillor Alan Hope commented that 'Neil Kinnock must be the only leader in British political history whose supporters have to be paid to hear him speak.'

I am totally baffled by an advertisement in the *Wokingham Times* in January 1981. A council employee was needed. The advertisement read: 'Requirement for a part-time handyperson or woman to undertake a variety of odd jobs around the premises. . . '

Gloucester City Council sent a 13p stamped letter to Mrs Lily Thomsett, demanding that she must pay her rate arrears – which amounted to exactly 2p.

Mr Philip Cabozet, of Collingham in Yorkshire, went on a shopping expedition to Wakefield in December 1983. He was refused permission to buy a clock in Boots, because of a council ruling that Boots were not allowed to sell clocks on a Wednesday afternoon.

According to Press reports, Mr Tony Banks, a GLC councillor, has been responsible for several laudable developments. For example, he has closed the champagne bar at the Festival Hall as being élitist; complained that the Coal Board was using cardboard cutouts of fake miners going back to work during the strike; taken down the Queen's portrait from Lambeth Council staircase because the royal family represents 'something to which Socialism should be totally opposed'; and, like Mr Kinnock, criticized 'The Archers' as being Tory propaganda.

In 1982 a new Town Hall was built by the Tory-controlled Royal Borough of Kensington and Chelsea at a cost of £14,000,000. The old Town Hall was then offered for sale for redevelopment. Then the Labour-controlled GLC started to think. If the Kensington and Chelsea council could not recoup some of their money by the redevelopment of the old site, they would be in an embarrassing situation with the ratepayers. Accordingly, the GLC prepared a Preservation Order round the whole of the old Town Hall.

Quick action was called for. All through the night of 11 June 1982, workmen toiled on behalf of the Kensington and Chelsea Council. When the early morning shoppers arrived on the streets on the following morning, all that they found left of the old Town Hall was a pile of rubble. Local residents protested. The GLC protested about the philistine destruction of an important piece of architecture (even though it had once been described as a Victorian monstrosity). The London and national newspapers protested. The Kensington and Chelsea Council rode the storm; they had solved their most awkward problem – the financial one. The site was bought for an undisclosed sum.

The London School of Economics is well in line with current trends. The Students Union has now decided to outlaw leering. A reporter from the *Mail on Sunday* went to assess the situation, and an LSE porter helped by demonstrating a leer, but a Students' Union representative was not so affable. 'I don't think this is very helpful,' she snapped, and left it at that.

A blue light used to be switched on over Southampton's clock tower every time the Tory council was sitting. When Labour took over, the blue light was replaced by a red one. 'It cost us only £39.44, plus VAT,' said a council spokesperson.

In Camden, the Russians wanted to build a wall of bluish-grey brick to replace a dilapidated wooden fence at their trade delegation in Highgate. The council, however, insisted that it must be red.

In September 1984, the Hackney Council replaced traditional oil lamps with battery ones, to cut costs. However, they bowed to Union demands for a compensatory payment of £925 for each of the twenty-two sewage maintenance workers who attended to the lamps. The total costs, including administration, amounted to £24,217, which was more than would have been swallowed up by two years of the old system.

In 1984 the Torquay Gas Board wrote to 'Mrs Smith, Deceased' (she had died the previous June) inviting her to spend the winter in 'a tropical paradise' for only £99.*

In May 1984 it was announced that the South Yorkshire County Council are to support Nipsy Championships on the rates. This is described as a 'working-class culture'. £300 was spent on advertizing, and there was £300 prize money. The nipsy, a small chock of wood, is balanced on a brick and then flicked into the air with the nipsy-stick and cracked into the distance. Any contender for the world crown should knock his nipsy at least 200 yards. Committee chairman Mr Jack Brown said, 'It's a game of great skill, far superior to golf.'

In April 1985 Camden Council brought an American artist to the borough, at a cost of £850, to teach children how to draw graffiti. This was part of a Hip Hop Festival, costing £17,000.

The Labour Research Department of the ILEA is producing a book based loosely on George Orwell's *Animal Farm* – only this time Rosa the pig, Clara the horse and Arthur the ram organize a strike against the farmer, Mr Moneybags. I am glad to say that the animals win their battle, and live happily ever after.

* For the only time in this book, I have altered the name.

A new pack of cards has been produced by the artist, Ms Cath Tate. It is entitled 'Alternative Happy Families', and was put on sale in August 1984 at £1.95 a set to raise money for the magazine *London Labour Briefing*. Out go Mr Bone the butcher, Mr Bunn the baker and Mr Fish the fishmonger; in come Lucy the lesbian, Guy the gay bookshop worker, Carl the crèche worker, Patience the peace campaigner's mother, and other fascinating characters. According to the pack, Guy 'goes with Laura, Lucy and Gary'. Gary is a gay teenager; I have not been able to find out Laura's particular forte.

In May 1985 Mr Ken Livingstone, of the GLC, opened a new construction in Battersea Park – a 110-ft. high 'peace pagoda', built by the Buddhist monks of the Nipponzan Mychoji sect, to be maintained at the cost of the London ratepayers.

It is reported that Lady Yapp, of the Merseyside Council, has in the past backed a scheme to finance a yashmak factory to clothe the West Midlands Yemeni population, and has also wanted to send eight Birmingham teenagers to Ghana so that they could learn how to do the local rain-dance.

And as I don't believe anybody can possibly surpass that, it is probably time to bring this preliminary study to a close.

Long live all Twitmarshes!

Answers to Section 3
Numbers 6, 15 and 21.

I am absolutely fascinated by Numbers 9 and 23. Your guess may be as good as mine, or even better.

Answers to Section 8
I hate to tell you, but every one of these entries is genuine!

Answers to Section 10, Questions 1 and 2.
Irrelevant, as the factory promptly went into liquidation.